RUNES for:

Divination

(Advanced)

Books by R. Briski

RUNES for: *Divination* (Basic)

RUNES for: *Divination* (Advanced)

(Coming Soon)
RUNES for: *Talismans*

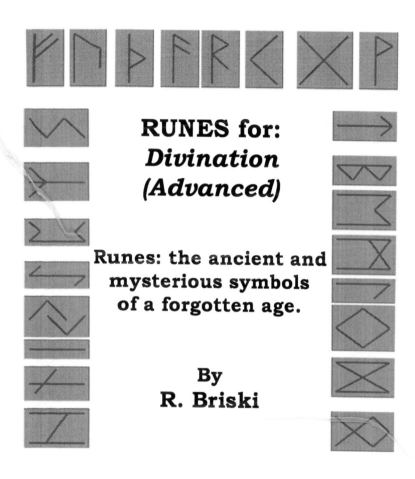

RUNES for:
Divination
(Advanced)

Runes: the ancient and
mysterious symbols
of a forgotten age.

By
R. Briski

ISBN: 978-0-9827921-1-7

Printed in the United States of America

Published by: www.SpiralJourney.com

This book is dedicated to
my ancestors.

OTHALA
*Awaken the Slumbering Dragon
of Ancestral Might*

And of course to my wife Astara,
without whom, none of this would have
been possible.

Table of Contents

RUNES for: *Divination (Advanced)*

Preamble

This book expands on the principles that were laid out in my earlier book, RUNES for: Divination (Basic).

It includes additional information about each of the Runes, a closer look at their meanings, and some advanced divination practices. Including, a more in-depth look at the use of Rune Tines in divination readings.

In this book I will focus on the usage of the Runes for Divination purposes. The use of Runes and Runic symbols for talismans I will leave for another time.

Rory Briski

Source

The word Rune comes from several ancient Germanic dialects and historically has meant "secret" or "mystery". The word root also has a vocal meaning of "whisper" or "roar". Therefore each Rune can be thought of as an individual unit of secret knowledge. With each unit of knowledge representing a unique mystery or principal of arcane lore.

As time passed, the Runic alphabet transformed from individual glyphs and symbols into a standardized alphabet that made words, sentences, and etc. However, this transformation did nothing to lessen the meaning of the individual glyphs, it only served to make their presence more obscure. Which is a good thing as this helped to protect the runic traditions from the invading religious zealots.

RUNES for: *Divination (Advanced)*

Origin of the Runes

It is through the Norse God of Magic, Odhin, that gods and men are able to receive the wisdom of the Runes.

Odhin was the first being to be initiated into the Runic mysteries by extracting the Rune wisdom directly from the source, and it infused into his being.

When the essence of the Runic knowledge merged within him, he was able to formulate the means to communicate their nature to other beings.

The shamanistic like initiation of Odhin upon the tree Yggdrasill is interpreted from the Poedic Edda, The sayings of Hár: "Hávamál", stanzas 138 and 139:

Rory Briski

I know that I hung
on the wind-tossed tree
all of nights nine,
wounded by spear
and given to Odhin;
myself to myself,
on that tree,
which no man knows,
from what roots it does rise.

Neither drink nor bread
they gave me,
I looked below me,
I picked up the runes
I took them screaming,
I fell back to the ground.

RUNES for: *Divination (Advanced)*

Brief History

The oldest Runic system, the 24 stave Elder Futhark, dates back to at least 200BCE (200BC). This set of ideographs was used extensively until around 800CE (800AD). Around this time, the Elder Futhark was slowly transformed into the Younger Futhark consisting of only 16 Runes. Also during the time of the Elder Futhark, an Anglo-Saxon derivative was developed that contained 28 Rune-staves.

These sets, and several other types of Runic systems, have been developed over the years but none have matched the pureness of form of the Elder Futhark.

Some books on Runes have also changed the original order of the runes, why this was done is open to conjecture, but I for one reject these random rearrangements.

For one, the name of the runes, "Futhark", is actually an acronym of the first six runes of the set: **F**ehu, **U**ruz, **Th**urisaz, **A**nsuz, **R**aidho & **K**enaz.

Further, the runes are in the order they are in not by whim of chance, but due to their specific meanings and how they relate to one another.

This book uses the original 24 Rune-staves, in their original order.

RUNES for: *Divination (Advanced)*

There is No Blank Rune

Runes are SYMBOLS. Have you ever seen a blank symbol? No? Neither has anyone else.

Runes are NOT the medium on which they are carved or drawn onto. They are the SYMBOL that is carved or drawn onto that medium. Symbols carry power, emptiness carries nothing.

As I'm writing this I look around the room and I see a blank notebook, is that a "blank rune"? Or how about the blank side of a garbage can, is that a "blank rune"? Or the blank wall under my window, is that a "blank rune"? No, no and no.

Some even attribute this so called "blank rune" to mean unknown mysteries or fate, which clearly shows they have no idea what they are talking about as this is the domain of the Rune Perthro.

There is no "Blank Rune".

RUNES for: *Divination (Advanced)*

Usage

Initially, the Runes were used singularly, as a pictograph or glyph, to represent some specific magical concept. As time progressed, the Runes were developed into an alphabet, but their magical significance was never lost. And eventually the Runes were combined into composite images to hold a higher esoteric meaning. Used as house marks or personal seals, they augmented coat-of-arms and heraldic symbols.

Their usage can even be seen today in some parts of the USA and Western Europe by the practice of putting a horse-shoe above a door for good health. The shape of a horse-shoe is basically that of the rune Uruz. A rune of Healing, Vital Strength and of the Homeland.

The two most common uses of the Runes were for divination and as talismans. As talismans they were routinely used to provide good luck, protection and offensive power.

When studying the Runes, each Rune is interpreted in a slightly different manner depending on if it appears in a casting of lots for divination purposes, or if it is inscribed on an item as a talisman.

While this book focuses on their meanings as tools for divination, a few words about their use as symbols of power is appropriate.

RUNES for: *Divination (Advanced)*

Talismans & Symbols

Used singularly, a Runic symbol has a great deal of force and power in and of itself. Historically, they are said to bring the wearer wisdom, wealth and luck. They were also used to offer protection from enemies and fears, or to give the wearer the strength to overcome them.

Talismans and symbols were carved on everything from wood to metal and from stone to bone. Swords inscribed with Runic symbols are common, as are bracelets and necklaces.

Several Runes used together, as in a bind Rune, provides an amplified power base. However, a great deal of care must be taken when creating bind Runes, a misdrawn composite could spell disaster for the Rune carver.

A sword with the Rune Tiwaz near the hilt. For victory and justice.

Many early graves had Runes carved into their stones. However, the most prolific medium was wood and bone. Both being easy materials to obtain and easy to work with. They also had the added bonus of once containing a life force.

Unfortunately, the ravages of time took its toll on the runes made of wood and bone. What we are left with to study are runes in stone markers and metal items. Yet occasionally, we see them in the wooden frames of building structures, in older places in Iceland, where the manufacture of home design is practiced in similar fashion to how it was done many centuries ago.

For the framing in some buildings shows clear runic patterns and yet serve no structural purpose. They build them that way because their fathers, grandfathers and great grandfathers built them that way. And so some of the lore is preserved even if they do not now recognize it as such.

The above is an example of a Talisman (Bind Rune) that I created for a non-profit organization. It was created with the following three Runes.

| Elhaz | Fehu | Wunjo |

RUNES for: *Divination (Advanced)*

ELHAZ: Communication Between Self & Higher Self, Spiritual Growth, Cleansing & Warding and Divine Communication

FEHU: Magical Force, Mobile Wealth / Mobile Power & Use Wealth (Money and Knowledge) Wisely and Generously

WUNJO: Self-Confidence in an Integrated Personality, Emotional and Physical Healing, Social and Domestic Harmony, Ideal Harmonization, Cope with or Elimination of Pain and New Social Relationships

BIND RUNE MEANING

Divinely protected and attaining the inner guidance, insight and wisdom to attract wealth and knowledge, in order to use it wisely and generously, to create emotional & physical healing and social & domestic harmony.

Divination

Traditionally, runecasting is a true act of direct communication between humans and the divinities of the many realms. The runecasters' will, ability, knowledge, level of being and understanding are all very important in interpreting how the Runes relate to the present situation.

When the Runes are thrown onto a table or drawn from a bag, it is thought that certain entities manipulate the Runes so they fall or are drawn out in a particular way. These forces could be manifest from the Great Norns: Urdhr, Verhandi and Skuld; or from other entities such as valkyries or the runesters' guides.

The oldest known method of divination was to cast the Runes onto the ground and without looking to draw three of them. In this type of reading, the order in which the Runes are drawn is very important, but whether they are drawn right-side up or upside down is of no concern.

The Runes as they relate to the three Norns are:

> The first relates to Urdhr: That which has become (the past),

> The second relates to Verhandi: That which is becoming (roughly the present),

> The third represents Skuld: That which may come to pass given past events (the future).

Runecasting is not so much an attempt to predict future events, but a way of attuning yourself to the web of interlocking <u>potential</u> futures that are woven all around us.

RUNES for: *Divination (Advanced)*

The most likely future course or event may become clear, based on what has transpired in the past, if no other course of action is undertaken to change it.

The ancients considered the future to always be in motion, and the future was shaped by past events. Remember, the present is only here for a fleeting moment, we are always moving into the future from an ever growing past.

Rory Briski

The 3 Aettir

The Elder Futhark is divided into three groups of eight Runes each. These groups are called aettir.

Each set of eight runes, derive their group name, or aett name, from the god/goddess that holds sway over the first Rune of that set.

The first eight runes are called Freyja's aett, for the Goddess Freyja. Freyja is a goddess associated with love, beauty, fertility, gold, magic, war and death. This aett symbolizes the creation of the cosmos, order out of chaos and creation.

The second eight runes are called Heimdall's aett. Heimdall guards the Bifrost bridge which connects Midgard (Earth) and Asgard (the place of gods).

RUNES for: *Divination (Advanced)*

This aett symbolizes forces that disrupt the patterns of the first aett and can cause great change.

The last eight runes are called Tiwaz's aett after the God Tyr. Tyr is the god of law and justice as well as heroism in battle. This aett is essentially the aett of the gods and divinity.

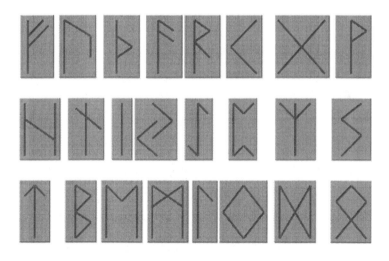

The Three Aettir

Rory Briski

Runes and their Meanings

As each rune is described in the next section, you will see the following:

➢ The name of the aett the Rune belongs to and its position in the aett
➢ If there is an element (Earth, Air, Fire, Water) associated with it, not all runes have these associations
➢ A drawing of the Rune
➢ Several historical associations or meanings of the Rune (with the one in italics being the most common meaning)
➢ Positive/Negative aspects are listed and are consulted depending on the other aspects in the reading
➢ Common Question Interpretations

The four most common types of questions asked in a divination reading are about: Money, Health, Career and Relationships.

RUNES for: *Divination (Advanced)*

After each Rune, I have included a short interpretation for each of these four types of questions.

Information about casting the Runes and using them for a divination reading can be found immediately after the sections describing the Runes.

Detailed information about how to interpret the Runes when using Rune Tines and their more complex interrelationships will be addressed later in this book.

Rory Briski

Freyja's Aett

The first aett is called Freyja's aett. It is formed of the essential elements and abilities that the runester must have developed within him or herself.

This aett is most aligned with the origins of the cosmos. Beginning with basic energy and continuing on with the ability to control, shape and use these energies:

➤ Magical force (fehu)
➤ Vital shaping power (uruz)
➤ Dynamic / active force (thurisaz)
➤ Inspiration and magic-skill (ansuz)
➤ Rhythm and timing (raidho)

RUNES for: *Divination (Advanced)*

> ➤ Control of energies and the skill to craft them (kenaz)
> ➤ The ability to give and receive power (gebo)
> ➤ Self-confidence in an integrated personality (wunjo)

FEHU

Freyja's Aett: 1-1

Element: FIRE

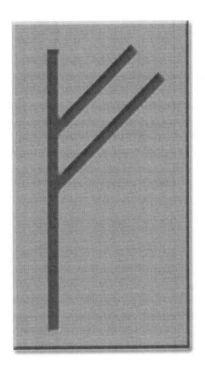

RUNES for: *Divination (Advanced)*

Conceptual Associations:

➢ *Mobile Wealth (Money, Jewelry)*
➢ Magical Force
➢ Raw Primal Energy
➢ Transfer of Energy
➢ Creation and Destruction
➢ Birth, Life, Death & Rebirth
➢ Fertility
➢ Libido
➢ Sexual Energy
➢ Use Wealth (Money and Knowledge) Wisely and Generously

Keyword Associations:

➢ Wealth / Poverty
➢ Sharing / Greed
➢ Excitement / Burnout

Rory Briski

Interpretations for a typical three Rune reading, where the seeker asks one of the four most often asked questions. These are "general" interpretations and must be tempered with the readers' skill and knowledge of the runes and their interrelationships.

Money:

> For Fehu to come up in a money question is a good thing as it rules mobile wealth, money. It also cautions to use money wisely and generously.
>
> I would say that if the seeker is lacking money then they should use money wisely and continue to spend, but spend prudently. Do not hoard it, but do not squander it either.
>
> If Fehu comes up in the Skuld position (Future) it is a very good sign of things to come with regards to money.

RUNES for: *Divination (Advanced)*

Health:

There are raw primal energies at work with this Rune and the ability to create and destroy is evident. Beware of burnout. Take a rest.

As a Rune indicating the cycle of birth, life, death and rebirth it may indicate a serious condition. Other Runes in the spread would have to be consulted for additional meanings.

Career:

Fehu here is about power, energy and having the power to create what you want. This Rune is telling you not to be passive, you must be active to get what you want.

Relationships:

Sexual energy, the libido, fertility, raw primal energy, passion...

Do I really have to spell this one out for you?

Rory Briski

URUZ

Freyja's Aett: 1-2

Element: WATER

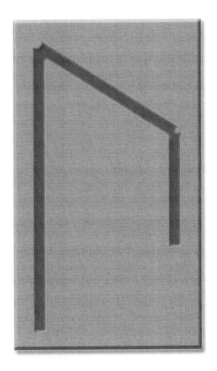

RUNES for: *Divination (Advanced)*

Conceptual Associations:

➢ *Vital Shaping Power*
➢ Homeland
➢ Rune of Healing
➢ Vital Strength
➢ Organic Life Energy
➢ Powerful Shaping Energies

Keyword Associations:

➢ Strength / Weakness
➢ Health / Sickness
➢ Understanding / Ignorance
➢ Homeland Defense / Obsessive Possessiveness

Rory Briski

Interpretations for a typical three Rune reading, where the seeker asks one of the four most often asked questions. These are "general" interpretations and must be tempered with the readers' skill and knowledge of the runes and their interrelationships.

Money:

Money must be used to shape the future you want to have. Money in or for the home is most likely what this rune represents.

Health:

For Uruz to come up in a Health question is a good thing as it rules Healing, as well as organic life energies. Vital strength is either needed or will be granted.

RUNES for: *Divination (Advanced)*

Career:

If you are currently employed, guard your job. If you are seeking employment, visualize, storyboard and create the energies that will bring you your goal.

Relationships:

Home, health and energy. This is not the rune of raw passion like Fehu, it is a rune of nurturing, understanding and strength. There are powerful energies at work here but the power of mutable water, not the power of burning fire.

Rory Briski

THURISAZ

Freyja's Aett: 1-3

Element: NONE

RUNES for: *Divination (Advanced)*

Conceptual Associations:

> * *(Aimed/Focused) Might & Melding*
> * Revenge
> * Mighty Warding
> * Dynamic Active Force
> * Danger May be Present
> * Reaction to Your Deeds May be Dangerous
> * Transformation of Force into Kinetic Energy
> * Rune of Crisis and a Catalyst for Change

Keyword Associations:

> * Reactive Force / Defenselessness
> * Vital Eroticism / Compulsion
> * Directed Force / Dullness

Rory Briski

Interpretations for a typical three Rune reading, where the seeker asks one of the four most often asked questions. These are "general" interpretations and must be tempered with the readers' skill and knowledge of the runes and their interrelationships.

Money:

> Be careful, very careful. The old saying from a pauper to a prince or a price to a pauper may apply here. You have the ability to channel a great deal of directed energy toward your goals, just be careful what impact your goals may have on others.

Health:

> This signifies the conversion of energy into action. Be careful not to overdo it. Plan to act and then act with force and/or determination. The "reaction to your deeds may be dangerous" may apply here. Take care of your body and it will take care of you.

RUNES for: *Divination (Advanced)*

Career:

> You may have felt threatened or attacked in some way and are now taking action against others. This could backfire on you so you may want to rethink your plan of action.

Relationships:

> Be careful that your focus and drive don't alienate people close to you. Also, don't let the vital eroticism of your current nature turn into a compulsion.

ANSUZ

Freyja's Aett: 1-4

Element: AIR

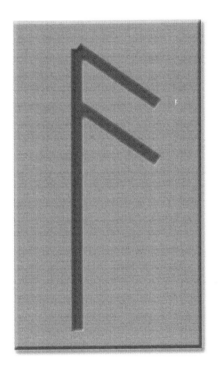

RUNES for: *Divination (Advanced)*

Conceptual Associations:

- ➤ *Creative Inspiration*
- ➤ Magic Skill
- ➤ Divine Conscious Power
- ➤ Power of Persuasion (Words)
- ➤ Responsibility to Ancestors
- ➤ Self-Transformation
- ➤ Expect the Unexpected
- ➤ Beware of Manipulation
- ➤ Bring Together Separate Elements to Understand

Keyword Associations:

- ➤ Inspiration / Misunderstanding
- ➤ Transformation / Manipulation
- ➤ Synthesis / Delusion

Interpretations for a typical three Rune reading, where the seeker asks one of the four most often asked questions. These are "general" interpretations and must be tempered with the readers' skill and knowledge of the runes and their interrelationships.

Money:

If you are expecting an inheritance, don't squander it. This could also relate to money coming from an unexpected place.

Health:

Self-Transformation is the key here. Don't just wait for others to come in and heal you. You must take an active role in what is happening.

RUNES for: *Divination (Advanced)*

Career:

To get ahead you will need to use the power of persuasion, as in talking about the issues and explaining why you are the best person for the job at hand. There are a lot of things going on right now and you must step back and look at them as a whole and bring them together to understand their meaning.

Relationships:

Be creative, unexpected, inspired. Relationships can be transformed if you transform yourself first. However, beware of manipulation here, the changes you make to yourself or your behavior should be made because "you" want to make them. If it doesn't feel right to you then don't do it.

RAIDHO

Freyja's Aett: 1-5

Element: NONE

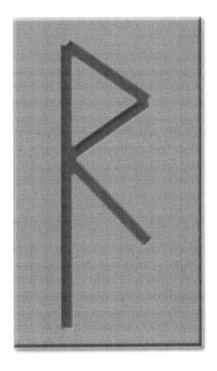

RUNES for: *Divination (Advanced)*

Conceptual Associations:

➤ *Rhythm and Timing*
➤ Ordered Movement
➤ Ward While Traveling
➤ Judgment – Soul of Law
➤ Long Journey – Growth
➤ Ordered Change – Action
➤ "Planned" Action is Necessary
➤ Beware of Bad Advice

Keyword Associations:

➤ Rationality / Irrationality
➤ Action / Rigidity
➤ Justice / Injustice
➤ Ordered Growth / Stasis

Interpretations for a typical three Rune reading, where the seeker asks one of the four most often asked questions. These are "general" interpretations and must be tempered with the readers' skill and knowledge of the runes and their interrelationships.

Money:

It should be coming, eventually. Look for slow, ordered growth of your finances. However, beware of bad advice that may derail or delay the slow and orderly growth of your funds.

Health:

It looks like it will be a long journey. No quick and easy fixes are indicated so you may as well enjoy the ride. Planned action is called for and necessary. You may be along for the ride but you are also in charge of the final destination.

RUNES for: *Divination (Advanced)*

Career:

Timing is everything. The long road you are on will have its ups and downs but you will get to your goal eventually. Just make sure you are heading for the right goal. Make a plan and stick to it.

Relationships:

This signifies growing and being together, although action is needed to keep things moving forward. Some kind of judgment may also be necessary. Base this on the "intent" of the person's actions, and not on the letter of the law or rule that was set down.

KENAZ

Freyja's Aett: 1-6

Element: FIRE

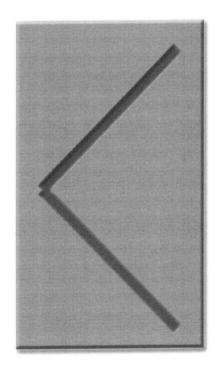

RUNES for: *Divination (Advanced)*

Conceptual Associations:

> *Shaping Things*
> Craft of Smith
> Transformation
> Analysis (Break into Parts)
> "Fire" of Divine Inspiration
> All Works of Knowledge into Action
> Rest and Relaxation Allow Creativity to Rise
> Control of Energies and the Skills to Craft Them

Keyword Associations:

> Creativity / Lack
> Offspring / Break-up
> Ability / Inability

Interpretations for a typical three Rune reading, where the seeker asks one of the four most often asked questions. These are "general" interpretations and must be tempered with the readers' skill and knowledge of the runes and their interrelationships.

Money:

Get creative on how to attract more money to yourself. Look outside yourself for inspiration. You have the ability to attract money, you just need to be creative in how you do it.

Health:

Time to rest. Use this down time to analyze your situation and formulate plans of action. Use the shaping power and fire of Kenaz to build or rebuild things in your life that are broken.

RUNES for: *Divination (Advanced)*

Career:

Analyze your current situation and break it down into its sub-parts. Look at these parts carefully to see how they can be transformed or crafted into energies, ideas, things that you can utilize now. However, don't get caught up in "analysis paralysis" so you never do anything. Look at what needs to be done and then do it. That is, take the knowledge you have gained and put it into action.

Relationships:

You can build whatever you want. Just be clear what it really is that you want to create and then apply the energy you need to make it happen.

Rory Briski

GEBO

Freyja's Aett: 1-7

Element: NONE

RUNES for: *Divination (Advanced)*

Conceptual Associations:

➤ *Equal Exchange of Energies*
➤ Love Magic
➤ Spend wisely
➤ Ability to Give and Receive Power
➤ Friendship, Loyalty & Hospitality
➤ Ritual Payment Must be Made (Give & Take)
➤ May Receive a Material or Spiritual Gift
➤ Expect to Receive or Bestow Credit or Honor
➤ Synchronistic Experience
➤ Do <u>NOT</u> Depend on Gifts

Keyword Associations:

➤ Generosity / Influence Buying
➤ Honor / Greed
➤ Magical Exchange / Dependence

Interpretations for a typical three Rune reading, where the seeker asks one of the four most often asked questions. These are "general" interpretations and must be tempered with the readers' skill and knowledge of the runes and their interrelationships.

Money:

> To get money you have to be willing to do something for it. There must be an equal exchange of energy/work for money to come into your space. However, a material gift "could" show up without the giver having any expectation of receiving anything in return. It's best to keep the giver in mind though and return a favor when possible. Also, try to spend wisely.

Health:

> Everything is give and take. What got you into the position you are in now? Bad food? Bad life-style? Remember, give and take. Try changing your old patterns to something that will give you the results you want. For

example, exercise and diet will help you lose weight. Cause and effect, give and take.

Career:

Loyalty and the equal exchange of energies is indicated. Expect to receive or bestow credit or honor on someone. Don't try and take all the credit for yourself if others are due their share. Do not depend on gifts to get you by forever. You must expend energy to get what you want.

Relationships:

If all you have done is give and not received anything, then you either gave in the wrong way or gave to the wrong person. On the other hand, if you are not giving but only receiving, you need to learn to embrace the equal exchange of energy with your partner.

WUNJO

Freyja's Aett: 1-8

Element: NONE

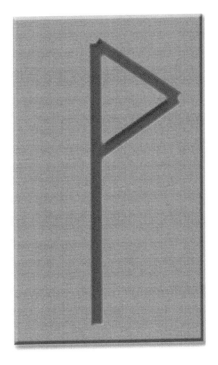

RUNES for: *Divination (Advanced)*

Conceptual Associations:

> *Self-Confidence in an Integrated Personality*
> Emotional Healing
> Physical Healing
> Ideal Harmonization
> Balanced / Integrated Personality
> Social and Domestic Harmony
> Cope With or Eliminate Pain
> Strive for Ideals
> Organize Things
> New Social Relationships
> Don't Lose Your Identity to Group

Keyword Associations:

> Harmony / Alienation
> Joy / Sorrow
> Prosperity / Strife

Rory Briski

Interpretations for a typical three Rune reading, where the seeker asks one of the four most often asked questions. These are "general" interpretations and must be tempered with the readers' skill and knowledge of the runes and their interrelationships.

Money:

Get organized. Balance your checkbook and know where your money is going. Prosperity is possible if you get organized.

Health:

Physical and emotional healing and harmony and the ability to either cope with or eliminate pain is indicated.

RUNES for: *Divination (Advanced)*

Career:

There may be new social and domestic harmony with new business relationships. Strive for your ideals but don't lose your identity to the group.

Relationships:

Self-confidence and balance should be your goal. New social relationships are possible. Social and domestic joy and harmony are indicated. Ideal harmonization whether with an existing partner or a new partner is possible.

Rory Briski

Heimdall's Aett

The second aett is called Heimdall's aett. It holds the Runes associated with the shape of the cosmos and the runester's initiation into higher levels of consciousness.

The energies of this aett are:

> The wholeness of universal structure (hagalaz)
> Testing to awaken the inner fire (nauthiz)
> Primal ice and the bridge of consciousness (isa)
> Cycles of the year and the growth of the seeds of power (jera)
> The vertical trunk of Yggdrasill and the initiation by ordeal (eihwaz)

RUNES for: *Divination (Advanced)*

- The Well of Wyrd and the ability of the runester to use its power (perthro)
- The Bifrost bridge and the communication between the runester and their valkyrja (elhaz)
- The wheel of the sun and the runesters magical will (sowilo)

HAGALAZ

Heimdall's Aett: 2-1

Element: ICE

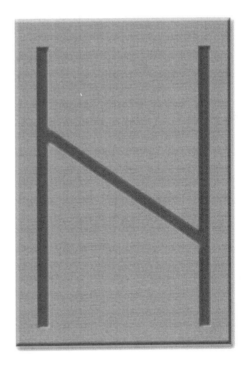

RUNES for: *Divination (Advanced)*

Conceptual Associations:

➢ Change or Transformation of Life
  Structure (Crisis or Trauma)
➢ Be Prepared for Crisis
➢ Wholeness of Universal Structure -
  "Hail"
➢ Mighty Warding Against Entropic
  Forces
➢ Completion and Bringing into Being
➢ Seed of Becoming – New Creation
➢ Develop Pure, Crystalline Ideas and
  Principals

Keyword Associations:

➢ Controlled Crisis / Crisis
➢ Harmony / Catastrophe
➢ Change / Stagnation

Rory Briski

Interpretations for a typical three Rune reading, where the seeker asks one of the four most often asked questions. These are "general" interpretations and must be tempered with the readers' skill and knowledge of the runes and their interrelationships.

Money:

> The message here could be, "be prepared for crisis". If you are ready you can control the severity of the situation, if not, be ready for some hard times.

Health:

> This Rune is about either tearing down or building up. Keep in mind that for a muscle to grow it must be torn down, via exercise, and then as it grows back it gets bigger and stronger. What aspect of your health can follow a similar course?

RUNES for: *Divination (Advanced)*

Career:

It looks like change and transformation of your life's structure are on their way, if not already here. Something big may happen soon that will change your perspective on the world. Something has completed and now it's time to move on to something else.

Relationships:

Develop crystal clear ideas of what you want and what you stand for. The seed of becoming or new creation is indicated. Could mean a new relationship or a new way of looking at an old one.

NAUTHIZ

Heimdall's Aett: 2-2

Element: FIRE

RUNES for: *Divination (Advanced)*

Conceptual Associations:

> *Strength to meet Trials and Overcome Them*
> The "Need" Rune
> Hysterical Strength
> Testing to Awaken Inner Fire
> Cause & Effect / Action & Reaction
> Turn Stress into Strength
> Necessity is the Mother of Invention
> Beware of Hostile Environment
> Danger on the "Easy" Path
> Unleashing of Potential Energy on All Levels – Energy Generated from Within

Keyword Associations:

> Strength / Constraint
> Innovation / Toil
> Self-Reliance (Need-Fire) / Drudgery

Rory Briski

Interpretations for a typical three Rune reading, where the seeker asks one of the four most often asked questions. These are "general" interpretations and must be tempered with the readers' skill and knowledge of the runes and their interrelationships.

Money:

> Necessity is the mother of invention. You need to be more innovative in how you are trying to acquire money. Turn your stress into the strength of determination.

Health:

> Beware of hostile environments. What in your environment can cause health issues? This is both on a physical level and on an emotional level. You have the inner strength to overcome any of these obstacles.

RUNES for: *Divination (Advanced)*

Career:

> You need to pay attention to the forces of cause and effect, action and reaction. Don't take the easy path, challenge yourself and know that you have the strength to prevail.

Relationships:

> It's time to rely more on yourself now as opposed to relying on others. You can carry your own weight, do what needs to be done, and come out ahead. Also, there may be a situation that develops that will test your ability to awaken your inner fire, or your passion.

ISA

Heimdall's Aett: 2-3

Element: ICE

RUNES for: *Divination (Advanced)*

Conceptual Associations:

- *Absolute Contraction & Stasis*
- Primal Ice
- Bridge to Consciousness
- Rune of Binding
- Stabilize Personality
- Unbreakable Will & Concentration
- Self-Control
- Unity of Purpose

Keyword Associations:

- Ego Consciousness / Ego-Mania
- Unity / Dissipation
- Self-Control / Dullness

Rory Briski

Interpretations for a typical three Rune reading, where the seeker asks one of the four most often asked questions. These are "general" interpretations and must be tempered with the readers' skill and knowledge of the runes and their interrelationships.

Money:

Contraction and stasis could indicate either nothing coming in for a while, or that you should stop spending so freely, or both.

Health:

Nothing gets worse, nor does it get better, it's at a standstill, stabilized. Use this time to bridge your consciousness and meditate on the issues at hand.

RUNES for: *Divination (Advanced)*

Career:

As part of a team you need to share a
unity of purpose or it will fail. If you
are looking for work there is
stagnation and lack of forward
movement. You must use your
unbreakable will, concentration and
self-control in order to break free of
the ice and move forward.

Relationships:

Possible stagnation and stoppage of
forward movement. Be aware of your
ego and self-control entrenching you
into a block of ice.

Rory Briski

JERA

Heimdall's Aett: 2-4

Element: EARTH

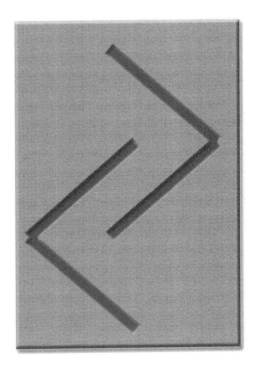

RUNES for: *Divination (Advanced)*

Conceptual Associations:

➤ *Patience and Awareness*
➤ Cycles of Year
➤ Material Well-Being
➤ Growth of Seeds of Power
➤ Rules the Creative Process
➤ Long Term Planning
➤ Reward for Right Action
➤ Expect a Good Harvest
➤ Aid in Growth of Own Understanding
➤ Beware Enslavement to Repetitious Behavior

Keyword Associations:

➤ Plenty / Poverty
➤ Peace / Conflict
➤ Good Timing / Bad Timing

Rory Briski

Interpretations for a typical three Rune reading, where the seeker asks one of the four most often asked questions. These are "general" interpretations and must be tempered with the readers' skill and knowledge of the runes and their interrelationships.

Money:

> Material well being is indicated. You have done the long term planning and now it will start to pay off. Expect a good harvest for your efforts. There is plenty of money available or coming.

Health:

> It's about cycles. This coming cycle should be a good one for you. Just have patience and know that you have sown the seeds of peace.

RUNES for: *Divination (Advanced)*

Career:

Looks like you will be rewarded for your right actions. Either through monetary means or though a new job, or maybe a promotion.

Relationships:

Patience and awareness of your surroundings are called for. Beware of repetitious behavior, that is, don't get into the rut of doing the same things over and over again. Now is the time for some long term planning.

EIHWAZ

Heimdall's Aett: 2-5

Element: FIRE

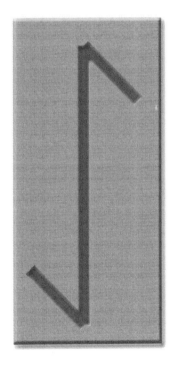

RUNES for: *Divination (Advanced)*

Conceptual Associations:

- ➤ *Connects Above & Below*
- ➤ Initiation By Ordeal
- ➤ Connects Life & Death
- ➤ Speak with the Dead
- ➤ Initiate Controlled Changes
- ➤ Beware of Burn-out
- ➤ The Vertical Trunk of the World-Tree Yggdrasill
- ➤ Mental Toughness and Flexibility are Needed
- ➤ Rune of Will That Survives Death & Rebirth Again & Again

Keyword Associations:

- ➤ Enlightenment / Confusion
- ➤ Protection / Destruction
- ➤ Endurance / Weakness

Interpretations for a typical three Rune reading, where the seeker asks one of the four most often asked questions. These are "general" interpretations and must be tempered with the readers' skill and knowledge of the runes and their interrelationships.

Money:

> This one doesn't come up very often in questions about money. If it does, I'd have to say hold on to what you have for the time being. Check-in with your higher self and meditate to get clarity. Protection of what you have may be indicated.

Health:

> It looks like the "Initiation by Ordeal" may apply here. Something is happening for a purpose. Possibly to aid you in connecting with your higher self or higher spiritual beings, or perhaps leading to enlightenment.

RUNES for: *Divination (Advanced)*

Career:

> Beware of burn-out. You need to have mental toughness and flexibility. Changes that are initiated must be controlled, and not chaotic or explosive. Endurance may be the key word for you here.

Relationships:

> It looks like relationships come and go into and out of your life and you have the strength of will to endure these activities. It doesn't mean that you will enjoy these happenings, just that you have the strength to endure them.

Rory Briski

PERTHRO

Heimdall's Aett: 2-6

Element: WATER

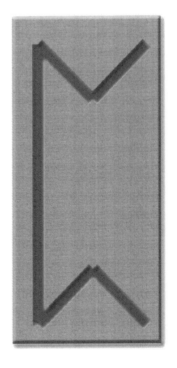

RUNES for: *Divination (Advanced)*

Conceptual Associations:

➢ *Well of Wyrd(*) and Ability to Use its Power*
➢ Rune of Divination
➢ Rune of Meditation
➢ Good Luck
➢ Fellowship
➢ Happiness
➢ Too Much of this Energy = Chaos, Destruction & Confusion

Keyword Associations:

➢ Good Luck / Addiction
➢ Joy / Loneliness
➢ Evolving / Stagnation

(*) Well of Wyrd refers to Fate and Personal Destiny. Here it signifies the ability to perceive and/or write your own destiny.

Rory Briski

Interpretations for a typical three Rune reading, where the seeker asks one of the four most often asked questions. These are "general" interpretations and must be tempered with the readers' skill and knowledge of the runes and their interrelationships.

Money:

> Perthro is the Rune of the dice cup, gambling, good luck, etc. Now may be the time to take a risk or a little gamble. Go ahead and roll the dice or buy that Lotto ticket and see what happens.

Health:

> While gambling and risk taking is a key element of this Rune, too much of this energy may result in chaos, destruction and confusion. Keep your risks to a manageable level.

RUNES for: *Divination (Advanced)*

Career:

Take the risk. Go for it. It may be out of your comfort zone but good things may happen if you branch out. When in doubt, try meditating on your question.

Relationships:

Risk taking, in moderation, may result in happiness, joyfulness and a fair amount of fellowship. Use the energy of this Rune to help you evolve into something you have only imagined in the past.

Rory Briski

ELHAZ

Heimdall's Aett: 2-7

Element: FIRE

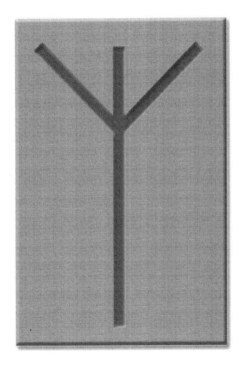

RUNES for: *Divination (Advanced)*

Conceptual Associations:

➤ *Communication Between Self and Higher-Self*
➤ Spiritual Growth
➤ Rune of Cleansing & Warding
➤ Used to Fare through Worlds
➤ Divine Forces are at Play
➤ The Bifrost Bridge
➤ Divine Communication is Indicated, Be Wary

Keyword Associations:

➤ Connection with the Gods / Loss of Divine Link
➤ Protection / Hidden Danger

Rory Briski

Interpretations for a typical three Rune reading, where the seeker asks one of the four most often asked questions. These are "general" interpretations and must be tempered with the readers' skill and knowledge of the runes and their interrelationships.

Money:

> Out of your control at the moment. Protect what you have. There is some kind of Divine lesson to be learned here.

Health:

> Spiritual growth and cleansing. This may indicate that you need to do a physical DeTox or cleanse, (consult with your doctor before doing anything). Or it could be more spiritual or emotional in nature, clear out all of the bad energy and make room for the good energy.

RUNES for: *Divination (Advanced)*

Career:

Outside forces, or your higher-self, have been at play here. What are they trying to tell you? Why are you in the situation you are in? What do you need to learn?

Relationships:

You need to check in with your higher-self, or your guides, or spiritual leaders and see if what you are doing is on the right path.

Communication is the key word here. Make sure your intentions are clear and concise and there is no room for confusion.

SOWILO

Heimdall's Aett: 2-8

Element: NONE

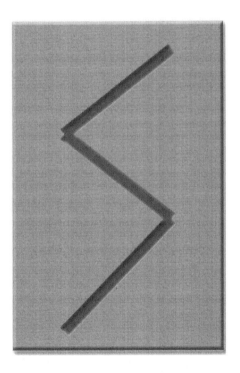

RUNES for: *Divination (Advanced)*

Conceptual Associations:

- *Rune of Invincibility*
- Final Triumph
- Wheel of the Sun and Magical Will
- Invincible, Unstoppable Force
- Have Hope, Good Guidance is Being Given
- Fix on "Your" goal for success
- Honor & Luck
- Beware False Success by Dishonorable Means

Keyword Associations:

- Guidance / Gullibility
- Goals Achieved / False Goals
- Success / False Success

Interpretations for a typical three Rune reading, where the seeker asks one of the four most often asked questions. These are "general" interpretations and must be tempered with the readers' skill and knowledge of the runes and their interrelationships.

Money:

> Looks good! This Rune is about success and triumph and good luck. Something may happen that is going to make you very happy.

Health:

> Very good news. This is about "Final Triumph" so whatever it is that you are concerned about you should be able to overcome it. You are invincible.

RUNES for: *Divination (Advanced)*

Career:

You are an unstoppable force. You need to fix on "your" goal, not the goals that others want you to have if you really want to be successful. You have honor and luck on your side so go for it. However, beware of achieving success by dishonorable means, it will come back to haunt you sooner than you think.

Relationships:

The guidance you are getting from others is sound advice. Fix on what you want your goal to be and go for it. Your goal is definitely attainable.

Rory Briski

Tiwaz's Aett

The third aett is called Tiwaz's aett. This aett is associated with the gods. It is also about coming into your own power and seeing beyond your current, limited, perceptions.

The energies of this aett are:

- ➤ The Sky-Father and victory (tiwaz)
- ➤ The great mother, birth and death (berkano)
- ➤ Twin Gods and Kings (ehwaz)
- ➤ The godly might of men and women (mannaz)
- ➤ The power of life and hidden resources (laguz)
- ➤ The god's sacrifice (ingwaz)

RUNES for: *Divination (Advanced)*

- ➢ Transcendent completion (dagaz)
- ➢ The inheritance that encompasses all (othala)

Rory Briski

TIWAZ

Tiwaz's Aett: 3-1

Element: AIR

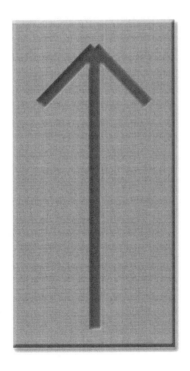

94

RUNES for: *Divination (Advanced)*

Conceptual Associations:

➢ *Justice*
➢ Victory
➢ Letter of The Law
➢ Spiritual & Moral Strength
➢ Stability and Ordering Force
➢ Strength, Courage & Honor
➢ Victory if You Acted Wisely
➢ Beware Planning & Never Doing
➢ Success Through Self-Sacrifice
➢ Faith, Loyalty & Trust in the Face of Hardships
➢ Strive for Precision and Plan Carefully

Keyword Associations:

➢ Justice / Injustice
➢ Analysis / Paralysis
➢ Self-Sacrifice / Over-Sacrifice

Rory Briski

Interpretations for a typical three Rune reading, where the seeker asks one of the four most often asked questions. These are "general" interpretations and must be tempered with the readers' skill and knowledge of the runes and their interrelationships.

Money:

> This is about the "letter" of the law and justice. If you are owed money you should expect to receive it. If you rightfully owe money, you will need to take care of that before you get into trouble. It's about having victory if you acted wisely.

Health:

> Victory over adversity. You must have spiritual and moral strength to overcome the odds. You must put forth the strength and know you have the courage to keep moving forward.

RUNES for: *Divination (Advanced)*

Career:

You will achieve success through self-sacrifice. You must also beware of planning and never doing. Don't get caught up into the "research" or "analysis" phase and disregard the "doing" phase. There has to be a time when you get up and actually go do something. Plan carefully and if you acted wisely victory will be at hand.

Relationships:

This Rune indicates stability and ordering force, and faith, loyalty & trust in the face of hardships. There may be some tough times ahead but you need to trust and have faith that things will work out positively. Plan carefully and trust that you will succeed.

BERKANO

Tiwaz's Aett: 3-2

Element: EARTH

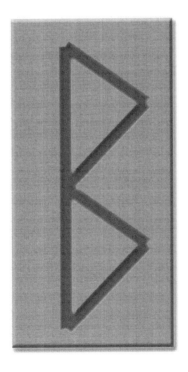

RUNES for: *Divination (Advanced)*

Conceptual Associations:

➢ *Birth and Death*
➢ The Great Mother
➢ Bringing into Being
➢ New Beginnings & Gradual Changes
➢ New Aspects in Erotic Relationship
➢ Prosperity and Beauty
➢ Beware False Appearances
➢ Look for Importance in Small
   Things or New Things

Keyword Associations:

➢ Becoming / Stagnation
➢ Birth / Sterility
➢ Shelter / Deceit

Rory Briski

Interpretations for a typical three Rune reading, where the seeker asks one of the four most often asked questions. These are "general" interpretations and must be tempered with the readers' skill and knowledge of the runes and their interrelationships.

Money:

> This is a good Rune for prosperity. Something may come your way gradually that will prove to be both beautiful and monetarily beneficial. But it will come into your space slowly, not with a big bang.

Health:

> Some aspects of this Rune are: birth and death and bringing into being gradually. A new part of you may be coming out and transforming, like the caterpillar into the butterfly. Or you may be giving a lot of yourself to nurture others. Look for importance in the small things and find joy in the newness of life.

RUNES for: *Divination (Advanced)*

Career:

> This could be a new business venture or a new position in an existing business but in another department or group. New aspects and bringing into being are very good career signs.

Relationships:

> New beginnings are indicated here. Most probably new aspects to an existing relationship or one that is just forming. Also, new aspects of an erotic relationship are also indicated. So, if you are not in a relationship now, prepare for a wild ride. If you are in one, well, same thing. Oh, and beware of false appearances; things and people are not always what they seem.

EHWAZ

Tiwaz's Aett: 3-3

Element: NONE

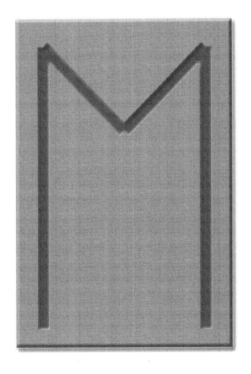

RUNES for: *Divination (Advanced)*

Conceptual Associations:

- *Teamwork (Horse & Rider)(Sword & Scabbard)*
- Twin Gods & Kings
- Power Under Guidance of Wisdom
- Telepathic & Empathic Links
- Harmonious Union of Dualities
- Dynamic Harmony with Others
- Formal Partnership May Be coming
- Accept Unique Differences
- Beware of Losing Self in Partner

Keyword Associations:

- Harmony / Disloyalty
- Loyalty / Betrayal
- Trust / Mistrust
- Teamwork / Duplication

Rory Briski

Interpretations for a typical three Rune reading, where the seeker asks one of the four most often asked questions. These are "general" interpretations and must be tempered with the readers' skill and knowledge of the runes and their interrelationships.

Money:

> This is about teamwork and partnerships. Money may be gained or may have been gained via partnerships that require or required "exceptionally close" teamwork. This super tight integration is required to further prosper.

Health:

> You need to use you empathic abilities and listen to your inner guidance and wisdom when receiving advice from others. Teamwork is critical for your success, as is trust.

RUNES for: *Divination (Advanced)*

Career:

Teamwork, loyalty, partnerships are vital to success. You need to accept the unique differences in everyone to achieve harmony at work. You can't do everything on your own, find someone to partner with. A formal partnership may be coming.

Relationships:

You need to find a partner that you can empathize with on a higher level. The teamwork called for is of two acting as one. The capacity to know what the other is thinking and acting on it is indicated. Just be cautious not to lose your sense of "self" in your partner. A formal partnership may be coming.

MANNAZ

Tiwaz's Aett: 3-4

Element: NONE

RUNES for: *Divination (Advanced)*

Conceptual Associations:

> *Blinders Will be Removed To See Things As They Are*
> Godly Might of Men and Women
> Melds Reason & Intelligence
> Strengthen Intelligence & Memory
> Awaken and Guide Psychic Abilities
> Happiness in Inner & Social Life
> Don't Dwell on Mortality & Weakness
> Beware Relationships Based on Lies and Misperceptions

Keyword Associations:

> Awareness / Delusion
> Intelligence / Blindness
> Divine Structure / Mortality

Rory Briski

Interpretations for a typical three Rune reading, where the seeker asks one of the four most often asked questions. These are "general" interpretations and must be tempered with the readers' skill and knowledge of the runes and their interrelationships.

Money:

> There is something that is hidden from you that will be revealed soon. Not necessarily hidden by others, it could be your own perceptions that are about to change. Thus letting you see something as it really is and not how you wish it to be.

Health:

> Don't dwell on mortality and weakness. Take time to strengthen your intelligence and memory, exercise your mind. You have the might of the Gods within you, use it wisely.

RUNES for: *Divination (Advanced)*

Career:

You need to be more aware of your surroundings and what is going on around you. Tap into your psychic abilities and temper your impulses with reason and intelligence. As was stated in the section on money, there is something hidden from view here that will be revealed to you when you remove your blinders and see it for what it is.

Relationships:

Happiness in your personal life and social life are possible. Just beware of relationships based on lies, half-truths and misperceptions. Use your psychic abilities to determine and know the truth.

Rory Briski

LAGUZ

Tiwaz's Aett: 3-5

Element: WATER

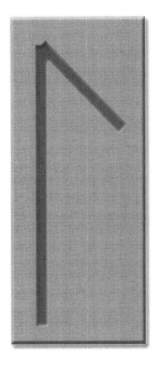

RUNES for: *Divination (Advanced)*

Conceptual Associations:

- *Physical & Magical Strength & Insight*
- Do Not Fear The Journey
- Life Brought from Darkness
- Hidden Brought into the light
- Power of Life & Hidden Sources
- Transition of one state of being into another
- Stern Tests in Life but you have the power to overcome them

Keyword Associations:

- Growth / Withering
- Vitality / Fear
- Journey / Circular Motion

Rory Briski

Interpretations for a typical three Rune reading, where the seeker asks one of the four most often asked questions. These are "general" interpretations and must be tempered with the readers' skill and knowledge of the runes and their interrelationships.

Money:

> This indicates stern tests in life but having the power to overcome them. Growth is indicated. What are you learning from this experience? Something is hidden from you and will be brought into the light for all to see.

Health:

> Vitality is indicated, both physical and magical strength. You do have the knowledge and insight to use them. Life brought from darkness could indicate a major healing or emotional breakthrough.

RUNES for: *Divination (Advanced)*

Career:

The messages here are: don't fear the journey and the transition from one state of being into another. You are being challenged now but you have the strength to overcome them. Learn from the challenges you face and keep moving along your path.

Relationships:

Growth, physical and emotional transformation and the power of life are all key associations here. Something hidden will be revealed into the light.

Rory Briski

INGWAZ

Tiwaz's Aett: 3-6

Element: EARTH

RUNES for: *Divination (Advanced)*

Conceptual Associations:

➢ *Converts Active Energy into Potential Energy*
➢ Have Patience
➢ Listen to Yourself
➢ Contained, Isolated Separation
➢ Rune by Which Power is Stored
➢ Active Internal Growth (Rest)
➢ This is a "Stage" not an "End"

Keyword Associations:

➢ Rest / Scattering
➢ Incubatiion / Impotence
➢ Internal Growth / Movement Without Change

Interpretations for a typical three Rune reading, where the seeker asks one of the four most often asked questions. These are "general" interpretations and must be tempered with the readers' skill and knowledge of the runes and their interrelationships.

Money:

> Have patience, action will come in time. This is not a rune that indicates receiving or spending a lot of money. It's a pause in the cycle of things to allow you to regroup and plan for the future.

Health:

> Your energy levels are being depleted. You need to store up your energy, like a battery, now is the time to rest and recharge.

RUNES for: *Divination (Advanced)*

Career:

Time for some active integral growth. The need to rest, be low key, passive and work on your inner being. If you have been seeking new work, now is the time to take a break to avoid burning yourself out. Look at what you have been doing and reflect on it. Is there another way to approach the task?

Relationships:

Have patience. It looks like contained, isolated separation is indicated. A time to be alone with your thoughts, to meditate, to rest, to reflect and to ponder. Listen to yourself and know that this is a "stage" and not an "end".

DAGAZ

Tiwaz's Aett: 3-7

Element: NONE

RUNES for: *Divination (Advanced)*

Conceptual Associations:

- *In the Light of Day All is Revealed*
- Meditation
- Achievement
- Transcendent Completion
- Enlightened Consciousness
- New Beginnings on a Higher Level
- Becoming One With The Universe
- A Great Awakening is at Hand
- Light Found Where You Don't Expect it
- Seek the Ideal

Keyword Associations:

- Awakening / Blindness
- Hope / Hopelessness
- Awareness / Deprivation

Interpretations for a typical three Rune reading, where the seeker asks one of the four most often asked questions. These are "general" interpretations and must be tempered with the readers' skill and knowledge of the runes and their interrelationships.

Money:

> Achievement is indicated. A great awakening is at hand. Perhaps you will receive money or perhaps you will discover that you didn't need as much as you thought. Something is hidden that will be revealed.

Health:

> Enlightened consciousness and transcendent completion are prominent here. There is some kind of breakthrough or achievement possible. Meditation is called for.

RUNES for: *Divination (Advanced)*

Career:

You should seek your ideal situation.
What do you really want? What is the
perfect resolution or outcome? New
beginnings on a higher level are
possible. Achievement is indicated.
You may find what you seek where
you least expect it.

Relationships:

You are gaining an enlightened
consciousness. You will find your
light where you don't expect it.
Becoming one with the universe may
be possible. Awakening must start
with awareness and hope.

Rory Briski

OTHALA

Tiwaz's Aett: 3-8

Element: EARTH

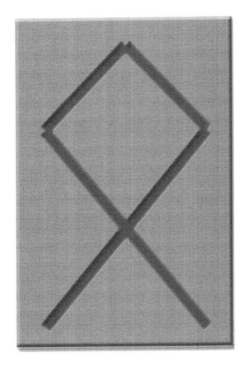

RUNES for: *Divination (Advanced)*

Conceptual Associations:

➤ *Rune of Inheritance & Power from Ancestors and/or Past Lives*
➤ Inheritance That Encompasses All
➤ Wisdom & Power from Past Lives
➤ Strengthen the Ties of the Clan
➤ Stable Prosperity & Well Being
➤ Attention to Group/Clan Customs
➤ New Dwelling or Allegiance
➤ Wealth of Possessions & Immobile Property (Land)

Keyword Associations:

➤ Group Order / Totalitarianism
➤ Home / Homeless
➤ Group Prosperity / Poverty

Interpretations for a typical three Rune reading, where the seeker asks one of the four most often asked questions. These are "general" interpretations and must be tempered with the readers' skill and knowledge of the runes and their interrelationships.

Money:

> Wealth is indicated here, though not in the form of paper money, but in the form of possessions or property. Such as by owning Real Estate, either a house or land. It could also mean an inheritance. In any case, stable prosperity and well-being are also indicated.

Health:

> Look to your ancestors for answers to your questions. Specific health issues may be hereditary so you need to know what your ancestors were afflicted with and create your own plan of action accordingly.

RUNES for: *Divination (Advanced)*

Career:

> You need to strengthen your ties with family and clan. Clan here could mean business associates, trade associations, clubs or groups you belong to, etc. Stable prosperity and well being can be found by paying attention to these groups.

Relationships:

> Use the wisdom and power from past lives, yours and your ancestors, to strengthen your group ties. Pay attention to "all" of the groups you are associated with and see what happens. A new dwelling or new allegiance may be possible.

Rory Briski

Rune Readings

There are several ways to conduct Rune readings and I will detail the two most basic methods here. These readings can easily be done using Runes with a variety of Rune shapes and sizes including ovals, rounds, squares, etc.

Runes can be carved into wood.

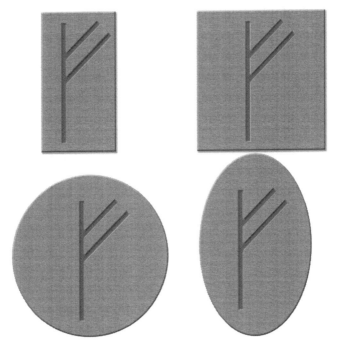

RUNES for: *Divination (Advanced)*

Runes can also be carved into stone, molded into glass/plastic or stamped into metal.

The Three Rune Spread

This type of reading appears to be the most common.

Place all of the runes into a bag and draw three Runes, one at a time. The order that the Runes are drawn from the bag is very important.

Alternately, you could dump all of the runes onto a table, turn them face down, shuffle them, and then pick three. Again, keep track of the order in which they are picked up.

Please note that there is no "reversed" meaning to the Runes. However, there are blockages and ways for some Runes to impact or impede others, but this is not typically determined from a simple drawing of a Rune upside-down.

RUNES for: *Divination (Advanced)*

As the Runes are drawn, they each represent in turn:

> ➤ The first Rune (ruled by the Great Norn: Urdhr) indicates the past. All of the things in the questioners life leading up to this point, or the root of the problem.

> ➤ The second Rune (ruled by the Great Norn: Verhandi) indicates the forces acting on the question and happening now.

> ➤ The third Rune (ruled by the Great Norn: Skuld) indicates what will happen based on runes one and two if nothing else changes. Staying on present course, continuing to do what you are doing, etc.

Example #1:

The person asks a question about finding a new job.

They reach into the bag of Runes and pull out one rune at a time. The Runes drawn are:

Rune	Name	Aett Position
1st	Elhaz	(2-7)

RUNES for: *Divination (Advanced)*

Rune	Name	Aett Position
2nd	Laguz	(3-5)

Rune	Name	Aett Position
3rd	Wunjo	(1-8)

Rory Briski

The Past: Elhaz indicates that divine forces have been at work or that the questioners higher-self has been influencing the situation.

The Present: Laguz indicates the person is currently going through tough times and tests but has the inner strength to overcome them.

A Possible Future: Wunjo indicates social and domestic harmony with new business relationships resulting in prosperity. Organization is also called for.

My Interpretation: I take this to mean that if the seeker gets organized they will find a new and prosperous opportunity.

RUNES for: *Divination (Advanced)*

Additionally, an equal number of Runes from each aett was drawn, one Rune each in this case, so it does not indicate any special attention needs to be put on any aett as a whole.

For example, if all three Runes came from the first aett, then that may indicate a strong influence of the basic and primal forces within the seeker.

Alternately, it could mean the raw abilities within the seeker. It all depends on the question and circumstances surrounding that particular question.

Example #2:

Assume that the seeker had asked a different question, but the same Runes were drawn as in Example #1.

The person asks a question about their health.

They reach into the bag of Runes and pull out one rune at a time. The Runes drawn are:

Rune	Name	Aett Position
1st	Elhaz	(2-7)
2nd	Laguz	(3-5)
3rd	Wunjo	(1-8)

RUNES for: *Divination (Advanced)*

The Past: Elhaz indicates that Spiritual Growth and Cleansing have been taking place.

The Present: Laguz indicates the person is going through a transition from one state into another.

A Possible Future: Wunjo indicates physical and emotional healing and harmony.

My Interpretation: I take this to mean that the seeker has been on a path of transformation and it is manifesting itself physically, giving rise to some uncomfortable issues.

However, at the end of the day, if the transformation continues, the seeker will have physical and emotional harmony.

The Nine Rune Spread

This is similar to the three Rune spread except that three runes are drawn for each of the time phases. That is, three for past, three for present and three for a possible future.

Each group of three Runes drawn is then read for each time phase.

This gives a more comprehensive reading about the basis of the situation and possible outcomes.

You may put the Runes back into the bag for each set of three draws. As previously mentioned, in rune casting, it is believed that the three Great

RUNES for: *Divination (Advanced)*

Norns (Fates) help guide which runes are drawn for each grouping.

The Past

The Present

The Future

Rory Briski

Runic Interrelationships

Interrelationships between the Runes can be more clearly seen when you look at the three aettir as a 3 by 8 matrix.

As previously mentioned, during the reading you want to watch for patterns to develop as to which aett the runes belong to, and which position within the aett they belong.

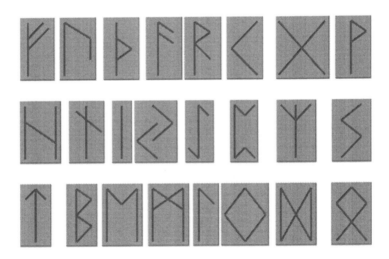

RUNES for: *Divination (Advanced)*

Look for a predominance of runes from a single aett, or from different aettir positioned within the beginning, middle or end of the aett.

Runes drawn from similar positions within the aettir show a special interrelationship and significance to each other.

These interpretations are in addition to those you receive for each rune in its individual position. They should be thought of as amplifications or clarifications of the individual Rune readings.

Three Runes From The Same Aett

With three Runes from the same aett present, all of the energies of those Runes are greatly amplified and the messages they give you should be taken in that context.

Three Runes from the first aett signify a great deal of influence from within the seeker. This signifies the seeker's ability to form, shape, control and use energy is very much in use here or should be in use.

Three Runes from the second aett signify a great deal of influence from groups around the seeker. This signifies that the seeker's ability to communicate both physically and spiritually is front and center and needs attention.

Three Runes from the third aett signify a great deal of influence from the higher planes of existence. This signifies that the seeker's ability to see beyond their current limitations and perceptions may be enhanced.

Of course there could be two Runes from one aett and one Rune from a second. In that case the two Rune aett would have a little more significance but not as much as when three are present.

Three Runes From Different Aetts, But In The Same Or Similar Aett Position

With three Runes from the same aett or nearly same aett position, it signifies an enhanced state of being or position in your life. The Runes should be read with the knowledge that there are additional forces acting on them and trying to convey a message to you. The reading should be made in this context.

Rory Briski

Three Runes from the beginning of each aett indicate a new beginning or stage of life.

Three Runes from the middle of each aett indicate: new communications, a journey or a transition.

Three Runes from the end of each aett indicate completions, healings or the end of something.

Rune Tines

Rune Tines are Runes that have been carved onto elongated sticks. These can then be used in more complex Rune readings and divination practices. Here is where the concept of a Rune showing up in a reading as more helpful or less helpful comes from. Not necessarily as "reversed" but in how it positively or negatively impacts other Runes in the reading.

For example, you could have ISA crossing FEHU, which could indicate a stagnation or blockage in money matters. Other Runes and their relation to each other would tell more of the story. All 24 Runes are used in these types of readings.

It is highly recommended that you become comfortable with the divination practices of the basic 3 and/or 9 Rune spreads before attempting divinations with Rune Tines.

An example of Rune Tines:

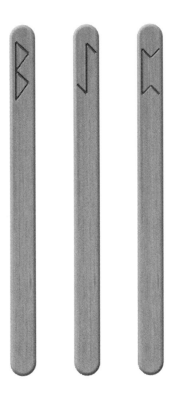

RUNES for: *Divination (Advanced)*

Readings with Rune Tines

A reading using all 24 Runes carved onto Rune Tines give the most comprehensive type of reading. It is also the most difficult and time consuming to interpret.

First, take all 24 Runes and place them into a suitable container. Then, the seeker should concentrate on their question and dump the container of Rune Tines onto the table

Only the Runes that have fallen face up are read.

Then the reader conducts the reading in several phases.

Phase #1

Look at which Runes are physically covering other Runes, even if ever so slightly. The more overlap, the more significance. Also, the greater the angle to perpendicular, the more the significance.

In this example the Rune Eihwaz is covering and is perpendicular to the Rune Berkano. So, it is in direct opposition to it.

RUNES for: *Divination (Advanced)*

Eihwaz is also just barely touching Perthro and almost directly opposing it but since the touch is light, so too is the opposition.

So, what does Eihwaz crossing, or in very strong opposition to Berkano mean?

Review the individual Runes with regard to the initial question, and what the seeker is asking for clarity on, let's assume it was about Career.

Their potential to bring into being new ventures, business or a new job are being blocked by their unwillingness to take chances or by their lack of mental toughness. Their state of mind may be confused and they don't see the direction they need to be going. They need to find clarity and should meditate or pray or whatever is it they can do to center their self and focus.

The tiny Eihwaz to Perthro blockage also reinforces the Eihwaz/Berkano blockage of risk taking and doing what they know they need to do to change or advance their career.

Phase #2

Look at Runes that are simply close to each other and note direction and proximity.

In the above example, Berkano is nearly parallel to Perthro but they are heading in opposite directions.

Berkano wants to "Bring into Being" and Perthro wants "Good Luck" and "Fellowship".

If they were heading in the same direction, that would be a very good thing.

However, with them heading in different directions, they have a negative influence on each other but NOT as much as if they were crossing.

RUNES for: *Divination (Advanced)*

Here I would interpret a stagnation in their career search or advancement as being caused by loneliness/depression, or an addiction of some kind. Whether that addiction is a physical one or a mental one may be determined by how the other 21 Runes in the spread fell.

Overall, how these three runes fell does not bode well for the seeker.

However, there are 21 other Runes Tines out on the table and you need to interpret them ALL to make a final determination.

Phase #3

Lastly you look for Runes that are lumped together by aett and aett position.

With only three Runes shown in my example it's difficult to display, but using the aett principals explained earlier, you may see patterns in the spread. But then again, maybe not.

The Fates decide the fall of the Runes and it may be that there is no overall aett influence in that particular reading, for that particular seeker, at that particular time.

I've seen many Rune readings start out looking very bad, as this one does, only to be very positive at the end should the seeker follow the advice that his/her guides are trying to bestow.

Remember, the Runes do NOT tell the future. They convey future possibilities based on what has happened in your past and what changes you make for the future. The future is always in motion and every action you take or don't take has an effect on what the future has in store for you.

RUNES for: *Divination (Advanced)*

Runes, Tarot & Astrology

While there is no historical evidence to support the old Norse or Teutonics believed in or practiced Tarot or Astrology, there has been some discussions over the past few decades about the Runes and how they relate to these other forms of divination.

It is possible to find some similarities in these other methods of divination and to the Runes, but these are really just aids in helping others that are more familiar with Tarot and Astrology get some "basic" concepts about using the Runes.

Just as there are many nuances and complexities in Tarot and Astrology, so to are there layers upon layers of meanings within the Runes.

	Rune	Tarot	Astrology
1	Fehu	Empress	Aries
2	Uruz	Chariot	Taurus
3	Thurisaz	Emperor	Mars
4	Ansuz	Hierophant	Jupiter

Rory Briski

	Rune	Tarot	Astrology
5	Raidho	Chariot	Sagittarius
6	Kenaz	Hermit	Venus
7	Gebo	Lovers	Libra
8	Wunjo	Sun	Pisces / Aquarius
9	Hagalaz	Tower	Uranus
10	Nauthiz	Chariot	Capricorn
11	Isa	Hanged Man	Moon
12	Jera	Wheel of Fortune	Venus / Libra
13	Eihwaz	Death	Scorpio
14	Perthro	Wheel of Fortune	Jupiter
15	Elhaz	High Priestess	Saturn
16	Sowilo	Sun	Sun
17	Tiwaz	Justice	Libra / Virgo
18	Berkano	Empress	Virgo / Venus
19	Ehwaz	Lovers	Gemini
20	Mannaz	Magician	Jupiter
21	Laguz	Moon	Moon
22	Ingwaz	Temperance	Moon / Cancer

RUNES for: *Divination (Advanced)*

	Rune	Tarot	Astrology
23	Dagaz	Judgment	Moon / Pisces / Neptune
24	Othala	Moon	Moon

Rory Briski

Thank You

Thank you for taking some of your valuable time and sharing it with me. I trust that this book has helped you to explore your curiosity about the Runes and I encourage you to delve further into their mysteries.

Please look for additional books in the "RUNES for:" series.

The author may be contacted via www.SpiralJourney.com.